Anonymous

The Story of John the Orange-Man

Anonymous

The Story of John the Orange-Man

ISBN/EAN: 9783744693660

Printed in Europe, USA, Canada, Australia, Japan

Cover: Foto ©Thomas Meinert / pixelio.de

More available books at **www.hansebooks.com**

THE STORY

OF

JOHN THE ORANGE-MAN

BEING A SHORT SKETCH OF THE LIFE OF
HARVARD'S POPULAR MASCOT

BY ONE OF HIS "FRINDS"

CAMBRIDGE

JOHN WILSON AND SON

𝔘𝔫𝔦𝔟𝔢𝔯𝔰𝔦𝔱𝔶 𝔓𝔯𝔢𝔰𝔰

1891

TO

JOHN LOVETT,

𝕳𝖆𝖗𝖛𝖆𝖗𝖉'𝖘 𝕺𝖗𝖆𝖓𝖌𝖊=𝖒𝖆𝖓,

*Who by his loyalty, his constant attendance at college sports,
his regular visits, and readiness always to "Trust
the gintlcman," has won the good-will of all,*

AND ESPECIALLY OF HIS "FRIND,"

THE AUTHOR.

INTRODUCTION.

TO begin with, why *should not* there be a biography of JOHN THE ORANGE-MAN? If thirty-five years of uninterrupted popularity at the first university in our land does not entitle one to a memoir, pray, what does? Half the men whose lives have been written have not even been popular for a single year. An humble position surely does not debar one from the privilege, for most of our great men, I believe, began their lives in log cabins, or on canal-boats; and who knows but what John may yet be a senator? An introduction seems almost unnecessary. You all know him!—Old John, who is the first to welcome the Freshman in the autumn, and the last to shake hands with the Senior on Commencement, and perhaps drink him God-speed from a flowing bowl of punch.   He well remembers the time your father was in college ; will tell you where he roomed, how he lived, who his friends were ; perhaps will even whisper in your ear of a narrow escape he had, in the early part of his Freshman year, from being asked to resign.   Is there a room in college that is not open to the genial bearer of the fruit-basket ?   Is there any one who has not tasted an orange or banana from the little white hand-cart ? Who has not been comforted, when sorely pressed by creditors, by John's ready willingness to trust him for any amount ?

How often on the ball field, when a game chanced to go against the wearers of the crimson, have we been cheered by a glimpse of a short, round-shouldered man, with a red fringe on his face, waving his cap and crying aloud for Harvard, in a voice rendered somewhat dim and moist by lapse of years !

Have we not been raised from fits of despondency, attendant upon some financial crisis, by John's evening visits, his good-humor, and his renowned song, " Erin-go-Bragh " ? Perhaps some of the more reckless of us have at times shared with him a " sup o' the bottle," partly to humor his sentiment of, " A drap av whuskey, av ye don't moind," and partly with a mild longing to get him into a convivial mood, and hear him sing.

But who is John the Orange-man ? Where did he come from, and how did he get under the wing of the Alma Mater ?

His life perhaps is not wildly exciting or romantic ; but must it be a closed volume on that account ? His sphere, though small and humble, has its interesting features.

In presenting the story of his life, I feel it necessary to make some apology for its

fragmentary character, in spite of a con-
viction that on general principles no book
should be published until it has been
brought into such a condition that no ex-
planation is necessary.   Most of the materials have been given me by John himself ;
some are new, some old.   I can do no
better than quote Bunyan's apology for
Pilgrim's Progress, — for the hero's life has
been a pilgrim's progress in a way : —

> " And so I penned
> It down, until at last it came to be,
> For length and breadth, the bigness which you see.
> Some said, ' John, print it ; ' others said, ' Not so.'
> Some said, ' It might do good ; ' others said, ' No.' "

The career of JOHN THE ORANGE-MAN
is before the reader.

THE STORY

OF

JOHN THE ORANGE-MAN.

———•———

I T was a Harvard Class Day more than
half a century ago. Cambridge was
looking its best, as it always does on these
occasions. The fifty-six members of the
class of 1833 were bidding their social
farewell to the university; the intellec-
tual farewell was to come some months
later, for Commencement Day occurred in
the autumn in olden times. This was the
class with which " Prof. Joe " graduated.

The celebration then was somewhat
more primitive than it is now. The graduating class was served with cake and

wine at the President's house, and then
marched to the chapel in University Hall,
where the exercises were conducted.   In
the afternoon there was the usual prom-
enade on the campus, and a punch, free
to all comers, was served on the shady
side of Harvard Hall. The materials for
this punch were brought in buckets from
Willard's tavern, now the car stables, and
the refreshing fluid was served to all who
might ask.

James Russell Lowell, in his article on
Class Day, says : " Nor was it an unheard-
of thing for bankrupt topers of the vicin-
age to circulate among the heedless crowd,
assuming an air of strangeness at each
return, thus repeatedly drenching their
adust throats, and blessing the one tap of
all the year whose waste was not scored
against them behind the door until it grew
inexorable."

But what has all this to do with my
story ? Nothing, except that at about the

same time that these festivities were going on, there was, on the other side of the globe, a smaller celebration in progress, the cause of which was the ushering into the world of the hero of my narrative. John the Orange-man was making his first feeble effort to fight off the grim spectre, and assert his right to live, move, and have a being. In point of numbers the rejoicing was small, being confined to my hero's immediate relatives, but was no less sincere than the great jubilee at Cambridge.

The scene of the event was the small village of Kenmere, in the southwestern part of Ireland, County Kerry. An unpretentious place it was, to be sure, situated on a small river near the sea, and surrounded on all sides by bogs and meadows. The houses, facing on a single shady street, were two-storied, whitewashed structures, with thatched roofs. At that time the place was noted for nothing in particular, unless the yearly exportation of a small quantity of peat is considered a noteworthy circumstance. Now it is celebrated chiefly, I fancy, as being the birthplace of John Lovett. If not, it certainly should be. Perhaps it is so far behind the times as to be wholly ignorant of the rise and greatness of one of its sons. But of this I am not informed, never having travelled through that part of the world. Here, then, our hero began the battle of life.

Like all the great men who figure in modern history, he was the son of "poor but honest parents." His father made a living by farming, hiring a place of some twenty acres a short distance from the village. The house was of stone, two stories high, with a pitched roof of yellow thatch. Behind it flourished a small kitchen-garden, while to the left was a stone cow-house, and the inevitable pig-sty. A hundred yards or so to the rear, and toward the river, was a small lime-kiln, from which a rough, worn path led to the quarry, a mile and a half away.

Farmer Lovett's revenue was derived from various sources, the earnings of the farm being swelled by the sale of peat and lime. Living was cheap, for milk and potatoes constituted the staple diet; and the expenditures for clothes and other necessities being small, the family was very comfortably situated. There were twelve children all together in the brood, — five girls and seven boys, — and they all played together, in a rural manner, with the pigs and the chickens, ignorant of the high distinction that one of their number was destined to receive.

John's early days were spent in helping about the farm, minding the cows, driving the donkey to the village with peat, and leading the oxen which drew the rude sledges from the quarry to the kiln. When eight years old, he was sent to the public school, which he attended for two years.

The schoolhouse was about three miles distant; and John had to foot it both ways. Moreover, each pupil was expected to bring two or three sods of peat to make the fire in the schoolhouse; consequently the privilege of receiving an education was something of a hardship to those living at a distance. John's only recollection of his scholastic life is that he studied a book called, "Radinmadeaisy," and "played thricks an the school-masther," who depended more on his stick than on his skill to impart learning and maintain discipline.

The surrounding country was rough, woods alternating with bogs and rocky pastures; and the boys used often to omit school from the daily programme, hunting rabbits, and setting traps for squirrels and other small game. John's particular pet was a tawny dog of no particular breed, and of doubtful pedigree; the creature, having a good disposition, however, and a fondness for rabbits and " sich-like," accompanied his master on all his expeditions. But life is not all play. When John was fifteen the famine came ; he was taken from school, and bound out to work. A hard life he led then ; no more sporting with the pigs or hunting with the dog, — only hard work and poor food. His father was obliged to give up the farm, and his brothers and sisters gradually died off until only two were left; they are still alive. One is a Cambridge milkman, and the other a baker in Memorial Hall. During the famine the oldest son emigrated to America, and found work in Waltham. Soon after, he sent for his mother, and two years after that John himself got ready to depart. He filled a small red trunk with potatoes, sifting oatmeal into the empty spaces, thereby economizing room, and packed what few clothes he had in a sack, because, as he said, " They wud sthale me pitaties, but wud n't tech me clothes."

There were no ocean racers in those days, and John was six weeks at sea in a sailing vessel. At first he was not happy. The rolling of the vessel was a new experience to him, and for some days but few visits were made to the trunk of potatoes. Gradually his appetite came back, and his face grew red and shiny once more.

The captain treated him very kindly, knowing that he was travelling alone ; and John was not at all backward in asking questions. He literally thirsted for information. " Is the rints hoigh, an' do there be famines, an' do yez know me brother Moike ? Do yez think Oi 'd be afther foinding iny gould av Oi wint to Califoorny? Is Califoorny near Barston ? Oi tink Oi 'll thry me hand wid a spade. Do yez raise pitaties over there, an' is the cloimate agreeable foor pigs? Yez ought ter say t'ould pig ter home ! She was jist afther havin' the foinest litter av kittens ye iver see, an' Oi hed to lave her behoind. Say,

did yez know Con Rafferty, as got the
gould midal for catching all thray av the
grayced pigs at the fair last soomer? He
was the handy bye wid the shillely too;
Oi've a crook in me nose now, fram a crack
he gev me thray years ago. Ye can fail
the loomp wid yer finger, roight here at the
top av it, capthain!" To all this the good-
natured officer listened with the utmost interest, and answered, to the best of his
ability, the numerous questions of his
ambitious protégé.

When the captain was busy about the
ship, John would sit by the hour in the
sunshine on a pile of rope, watching the
sailors at work, and dreaming about the
new country that he was fast approaching.
Day after day went by, and finally land
came in sight. The outer islands of Boston
Harbor were passed, and soon the smoke of
the city was visible. John was all eyes.
So many houses, so much smoke! he was
quite bewildered. The vessel hove to at

the wharf, and John stepped ashore, with his trunk on his shoulder, and his last potato in his pocket.

He asked a man the way to Cambridge, and started up State Street from the water-front. A curious specimen he was, clad in short corduroy trousers, black coat, and flat-crowned Derby hat. On his shoulder he carried his trunk, and in his hand was a stout blackthorn cane. He was twenty years old and penniless, but with a career before him. He strode up the street, past the old State House, stopping occasionally to look in at store-windows, or to gaze up at the apparently endless rows of buildings. Some street Arabs jeered at him, calling him "Irish," but fled as he turned and shook his stick at them.

How different was Boston from the place he had left! He had never seen a city before, and was half stunned by the noise ; the crooked, crowded streets confused him, and passers-by, jostling him, turned and smiled at the hopelessly lost expression on his countenance.

At length, after numerous inquiries, he succeeded in reaching the river-front, where he paused to collect his scattered wits. He seated himself on the trunk and wiped the sweat from his brow with a faded red handkerchief, which plainly gave evidence of having been recently in contact with the " pitaties." The cool breeze refreshed him ; and after a short rest he shouldered his trunk once more. There were few pedestrians on the bridge, and he got along faster. His spirits rose ; his journey was almost over, and he stepped along gayly.

Suddenly he was stopped by the words, " Hi there! toll! "

John looked around. " Phwat d' yer mane ? " he asked.

" One cent toll, or yer don't go over," was the reply.

John was puzzled ; they never did that

at Kenmere. He had been accustomed to go wherever he pleased without being obliged to pay for the privilege. He felt through his pockets mechanically, though he well knew there was nothing there but a potato, and then told the keeper of the gate that he had no money.

" Then you 'll have to stay in Boston," was the only answer he got.

John thought a minute, and then a bright idea struck him. " Oi tell ye how we 'll fix it," he said. " Oi go over now, and koom back ter-marrer and pay ye the cint."

" Not much you don't," said the keeper. " You can't come that on me."

Our hero's Irish ingenuity did not fail him at this. He was bound to get over some way. " Say, you mon, kin Oi koom over this half av the bridge widout payin' ? "

" Yes, of course, as long as you don't go by here."

" An' if I was on the ither soide, could Oi koom up as far as this widout payin' ? "

" Yes; but you'd have to pay to go over this particular ten feet of the bridge."

"Aw, will, if yez only hev to pay to go over tin fate av the bridge, Oi 'm arl roight. Oi kin joomp that aisy !"

The man laughed, but was relentless. Poor John ! so near his destination. He leaned over the rail and looked down into the running tide of the Charles. A sea-gull flew over his head, uttering its shrill cry. It was not the wild-eyed, storm-tossed gull that always flies over the desolate maiden, as she stands by the shore gazing after the ship that is bearing her lover away, but a plain, unpretending Charles River gull, whose highest aspiration was an oozy mud-flat, and who had never even dreamed of taking part in a romantic scene. John flung a stone at the bird, muttering something about a "fray kentry, where ye hed to pay to walk," and then seated himself disconsolately on his trunk. But what was he to do ? To be thus stopped on the very threshold, after his long journey, was a melancholy event. Cambridge was in sight on the opposite shore. A tear rolled down his cheek, and was lost in the fuzzy auburn beard. A passing teamster observed his plight, and pitying the forlorn alien, paid his toll, and drove him out to Cambridgeport. From there he walked to Harvard Square, passing the college yard that he was destined in a few years to patrol.

Several students laughed at him, but he was too intent on finding his friends to notice their jeers. Turning down Brighton Street (now Boylston), he walked toward the river.

"Hello, John! Phy, phwat a bye ye 've grown to be! Phy, Oi hardly knew ye!"

"Hello, Dan! it 's doom glad Oi am to foind ye!" He was in his cousin's arms, and his wanderings were over.

For several months he lived with his friends on Brighton Street, and then hired

a couple of rooms in the old Dennison
house on the corner of Mason and Garden
streets, where the Shepard Church now
stands.

He sent for his mother, who was in
Lowell with his brother ; and for seven
years they lived in these two rooms, for
which they paid five dollars a month. In
various ways he tried to earn a living, — did
chores, beat carpets, sawed wood, and did
other odd jobs for Cambridge residents.
It was an humble beginning ; but those
who are to rise must begin at the bottom.
John's promotion soon came. It was a
warm day in June — but, stay ! we will
have the story of his first meeting with
the "sthudints" in his own words : —

"It was a haŕt day, frind, about thray
o'clark in the afthernoon, an' Oi wint over
an the carmmon to wartch the byes play
barl. Afther they git through, they tell me
to bring thim some wather to dhrink ; an'
Oi wint over to me house and got a big

pitcher av wather, and pit some ginger
in it, an' some merlasses, an' a bit
av vinegar, an' some oice; an' I carried
it over to thim, an' they till me to git
thim another pitcher, an' Oi did; an'
they mek up a subschription av about two
darllers for me, an' Oi did n't want to
tek it, but they med me, an' Oi did!
Wan sthudint invoighted me down to his
room in Harllis Harll, an' whoile Oi was
there a whole lart av 'em kem in; an' they
gev me a carpet, an' some old clothes,
an' some shoes, an' they till me if I buy
fruit, and kem around to their rooms, I
could git along very will wid thim; an' Oi
did! an' they all buy av me. I used sell
'r'nges, 'n' b'nanas, 'n' candy, 'n' jew'lry.
They did n't buy me candy 'n' jew'lry much,
but they always tuk me 'r'nges 'n' b'nanas!
Some day I was mek about two darllers, and some day only sivinty-foive cints.
There was another man used go round
selling candy. He was called 'Jimmy;'

he was very ould and fayble, an' half bloind. He died a year or two afther Oi begin to go around ; he was a good feller, Jimmy was, frind."

For about six years John lived alone with his mother, selling fruit from room to room in the old college buildings. Then came his second promotion : he determined to indulge in the luxury of a wife. After due deliberation he set his heart on a certain charming Mary Hallisy, who lived on Brighton Street. His courtship was a short one, lasting only about two months, and then they were married. They lived on Brighton Street for about three years, hiring a room in his cousin's house. But the desire to own a place of his own at length took possession of John, and he determined to move. Moreover, as he says, " They did n't loike I be bringing so much fruit into the house, for fear I be hurtin' something." So he drew from the bank his hard-earned savings, and bought a bit

of land on Beaver Street, for which he paid
four hundred dollars. He filled up the
land himself with ashes, working every day
until nearly midnight, and then began to
build, doing much of the work himself,
at least such parts as required no skilled
labor. It is a double house ; and John
rents the other half, thereby helping out
his income considerably. Altogether his
house cost him thirteen hundred dollars,
and he mortgaged it for nine hundred.
It took him six years to pay off this mortgage ; and there was not a happier man in
Cambridge than Old John, when the last
cent was paid and the house was his own.
Some years after, the city raised the land,
and John had to hoist up the house, to
keep pace with the times, and prevent
passers-by from looking down the chimney.
This cost him seven hundred more, and
another mortgage was necessary, which was
not paid until about two years ago. This
change added another story to his house,

for he gave it a big lift while he was about it ; and what was formerly the kitchen is at the present time "the parloor on the sicond flure ! "

At all events, he is comfortably settled now, and has a snug little sum laid up in the bank against a rainy day ; for crises will come, even to the best-regulated business man.

In 1881 he was presented with a hand-cart by members of the graduating class and some others. Up to this time he had been compelled to lug his fruit in a basket ; and the cart was a priceless treasure to him. He says, " They warnted to give me a darn-key too, but I be afraid the Farculty mek a row about havin' 'im in the yard." It is hard to conceive what possible evil could have resulted from the advent of a donkey, except that the grass might have refused to grow in his shadow, for John is something of a barnacle during the day, spending most of his time on the sunny steps of

Matthews and Hollis. Among John's val
uables is treasured a paper, somewhat yellow with age, and a trifle torn and soiled,
bearing the following inscription : —

" We the undersigned, recognizing in John the
fruit-man an old 'frind,' and one who has sup-
plied the college with fruit for a quarter of a
century, and desiring to lessen the burden of his
heavy baskets by presenting him with a two-
wheeled hand-cart, in which to draw his baskets
from his house to the Halls and to Jarvis Field,
do hereby subscribe one dollar ($1.00) for that
object."

Then follows a list of some forty names,
headed by a now prominent citizen of San
Francisco.

The cart was duly purchased, and presented to John in front of Matthews Hall,
with ceremonies fitting the occasion.

Soon after this he had a slight misunder-
standing with the " yard boss," who finally
informed him that the authorities would
not allow him to bring his cart on the

campus, and that he must leave it at the gate. John retailed his woes to some of the students, who petitioned the Faculty to show clemency to the Orange-man ; and an edict was issued to the effect that John and his cart should not be interfered with. A delegation waited on the old fruit-dealer with this edict ; and he was borne in triumph through the college gate, cart and all, amid deafening cheers ! For ten years he has wheeled his fruit about the yard in rain and shine, and to all appearances the vehicle is as serviceable as ever. Starting from his house about nine o'clock, he spends the forenoon in the college yard, depending on stray customers between the recitations and lectures ; in the afternoon, if the weather be warm, he visits the ball fields ; while in the evening he makes his tours through the dormitories.

To those who know him well he is rather an interesting study, though his brogue is a trifle hard to comprehend at times. One of the best traits of his character is that he can never be induced to speak ill of any one. Mingling as he does with the men of various sets and cliques, he necessarily hears more or less slander, but if asked his opinion about a man, his only comment is, " Aw, he 's a good fellah, frind." To some few he occasionally confides his likes and dislikes, but in general is very non-committal. He hears and knows of many dark deeds committed within the college walls, but takes a legitimate pride in saying, " Oh, but Oi 'd niver till, frind, who done it; Oi could n't do *thot!* "

At times he is very sociable, and will make a long evening call, lighting his pipe, and sacrificing business to comfort. It is on these occasions that his interesting stories come out. He will tell about the old professors he used to know. Sophocles seemed to be one of his favorites.

" Ah, yis, frind, I know Sarphacles viry will. He was always kep' around his room

in Harlworthy, an' he buy fruit av me.
He kerried an ould grane oombrella, and
wore always the same ould hat. I asked
him one day why he did n't wear his good
clothes when he go to Boston, an' he say
the blacklegs would go for him, thinkin'
he be rich! He niver let the women brush
the carbwebs from his room, an' used sind
me over to the grain-store to buy grain fer
him to throw out to the sparrers for fear
they go hengry. He give me woine some-
times, but I did n't like it very much. He
pit some koind av spoice in it, and say it
was loike they do at home; he used carry
his own bottle of woine whiniver he go
out to dinner. He till me wanst that in
Grayceland he git a shave fer wan cint;
he niver git shaved here at all!"

Clery, the old negro who took care of
the chemical laboratory, and was commonly
known as "The Professor," was another old
friend of John. He died two years ago.
John met him when he was first connected

with the college, and the two used to chat together in the yard every morning.

On one or two occasions the name of John Lovett has been entered on the books of the district court. His first arrest was fifteen years ago. With a party of friends he had been making merry at a wake, or something of the kind, at Mount Auburn, and the crowd, being somewhat boisterous on the way home, were locked up for disturbing the peace. He escaped with a small fine. At his next appearance before the magistrates, he figured in the rôle of accuser. While passing through Church Street, he had been attacked by an irate driver, whose horses had taken fright at the hand-cart. A couple of students rescued him from the clutches of his assailant, who was subsequently arrested on charge of assault. John's case was conducted by a party of law-school men, who won the day for him. The driver was fined twenty dollars with costs, and John was marched away to the yard in triumph, where the victory was celebrated with appropriate rejoicings.

Of late years it has become the fashion to have John accompany the ball teams as a mascot. The first big game, outside of Cambridge, that he was present at, was the one played in New York in 1888. John went down with the crowd, and he and the students made things pretty lively on the boat. They sat on the upper deck, singing songs and telling stories, until nearly midnight ; and naturally John was the central object of interest.

His vocal powers are *sui generis.* He has a range of about half an octave, and it requires a good deal of skill to bring the average song within that compass. It is something like Chinese music ; one must be educated to it in order to appreciate it. His favorite song is " Erin-go-Bragh." The words I give as he renders them. I believe he does not hold strictly to the original.

" At first, in my youth, as I was spadin' the land,
  Wid the brogues on me feet, an' the spade in me
    hand,
The people they say 't was a pity to see
Such a hansome young man cuttin' turf in
  Truree.
I butter me brogues an' shook hands to me spade,
And wint to the fair loike a dandy arrayed.
Out came a sairgint who asked if Oi 'd list,
Av he gev me the shillin' he hild in his fist.
Erin-go-Bragh, — shillely and all, —
My heart it be wid you, oh, Erin-go-Bragh ! "

There are seven or eight more stanzas, but
I will spare the reader.

The night porter on the steamer evidently had not the same appreciation of
John's melodies that the students had, for
he threatened to put the soloist down on
the lower deck, if he did not " shut up." He
was informed, however, that if he did he
should have to put down about three hundred others first, and this job he was un-
willing to undertake.

On reaching New York, the mascot, arrayed in crimson scarfs and flags, was

taken all over the city and shown the sights. He dined at the Hoffman House, and in the afternoon was driven to the field on a coach, to witness the game. His excitement knew no bounds, and he wagered all the money he had with him on the crimson. Poor, hopeful John! he lost it all.

At the Springfield game in 1890 he was also a prominent figure. His appearance on the field was announced by cheers, and cries of "John! John!" all along the line. To these he responded by waving a couple of crimson flags, and shouting, "Hairvard! Hairvard!" He was immediately seized and dragged to the grand stand, where a seat had been reserved for him. A more excited or enthusiastic individual than John could not be found on the field, when the game closed with a score of 12 to 6 in Harvard's favor. He has always been a foot-ball enthusiast, ever since the days when the Freshmen and Sophomores cele-

brated " Bloody Monday " by a terrific
struggle on the delta, where Memorial Hall
now stands. People came from miles
around to watch them, and the fruit-man
was always on hand with his baskets. In
1860 these contests were abolished as
being dangerous ; and a foot-ball, enclosed
in an oak coffin, was buried on the field.
Speeches were made ; an ode was read ;
and a tombstone, bearing a fitting inscription was erected over the grave.

But I have dwelt enough on John's public life. Of his home life there is little to
be said. I shall never forget my first for-
mal call on the Orange-man. He had often
expressed a wish that I should " drap
around some day and hev a luk at his
place ; " and accordingly I set out, one
bright spring morning, armed with a
camera, to find his homestead.

The task was more difficult than I had
anticipated, and I soon found myself hopelessly lost among the amphibian streets of

lesser Cambridge, — Otter Street, Beaver
Street, and Heaven knows what others!
At length I espied a small mucker playing
shinney alone in a back yard, and hailed
him with joy: " Hi, you boy! where does
John live ? "

" John Lovett, ye mane ? " asked the boy,
pausing a moment in his exciting sport,
and eying me with mingled awe and
curiosity.

" Yes, of course ; what other John is
there ? "

The boy pointed down the street with
his shinney stick, and said, " Over in that
yaller house."

I crossed over, with some incredulity.
Could it be possible that this substantial
three-story house had been raised with
the proceeds of the sale of " 'r'nges 'n'
b'nanas " ? Before I could open the gate
John himself was at the door. " How do
you do, frind ? Come roight in an' mek
yourself to home."

I entered the kitchen, and was formally introduced to his wife, who greeted me with a " Gud-*manin*, sur ; it's a fine *manin*, sur." Seating myself in an armchair by the stove, I looked about. A bright fox-terrier capered around with one ear erected on the alert for anything interesting; a plump Maltese cat rubbed sociably against my leg, and then hastened to answer the call of a small kitten that was trying to crawl out of a saucer of milk. Everything was very home-like. Mrs. John bustled about, and insisted on my having "a couple av biled eggs, and a sup av tay." The kitten, now rescued from its predicament, was dragging itself along toward the stove, leaving little blue trails on the floor, which the mother neatly lapped up. Great interest in the proceedings was shown by the terrier, who trotted around with a knowing air, occasionally suggesting by a sharp bark that his wants had not been attended to.

John did not propose to have his guest

annoyed by any such manners, and accordingly ejected the dog, remarking, " Go an
out, Spart, an' doan't be a-bairkin' at the
gintleman."

"What do you call him, Spot or Sport ?'
I inquired mildly.

" Spart, frind," replied John, in his be-
wildering brogue.

What an ambiguous name!

I was then taken up to the parlor, which
is over the kitchen, and shown all the family treasures. A large photograph album
was brought out which contained many of
John's " frinds." Prominent graduates and
their sons were side by side. A well-known
'86 man was on the page directly opposite
a dime-museum Abyssinian woman with a
shock of hair as large as a bushel-basket,
and bedecked from head to foot with tin
ornaments and what Kipling calls " open-
work jam-tart jewelry ! " The celebrated
Harvard athlete, a record-holder, was side
by side with the variety-show gymnast,

who wore a score or so of medals, badges, and other trophies pinned on his jersey.

I hinted to John that it would be pleasant if he could have another album, and keep all the " college gintlemin " together, and he seemed to think the idea a good one. " I niver think av that, frind ; I think I will. I 've a lart more av 'em away in a thrunk."

The parlor was prettily furnished with a square piano, sofa, centre-table, easy-chairs, and numerous smaller pieces. Over the centre-table hung a chandelier gorgeous with glass prisms of rainbow hues, while on the walls hung various pictures, a " God-bless-our-home " worked with colored worsted on a colander background, and other *bric-à-brac.*

" Is this where you spend your leisure, John ? " I asked.

" No, frind ; I be doun in the kitchen wid Mary most av the toime. It feel more ter home doun there."

He evidently prefers the bare kitchen, with its one broken-down armchair, and comfortable cook-stove, to the cosey parlor above, which is used as a reception-room.

After going over the house, we inspected the live-stock. He has a promising flock of hens, in which he takes great pride.

I was very anxious to secure a picture of the old man feeding his fowls, and at the last minute conceived the daring project of getting a likeness of Mrs. J. I whispered to John, and he went into the house to get his better half.

I heard him trying to persuade her, and then came her protest in a high-pitched, rapid voice: "Oi will nart, Jan. Oi won't, Oi till ye! It's oogly enough Oi be widout havin' any pictur or foolishness tuk, for any av yer ould buk, so there, Jan; an' ye lave me be, fur Oi don't go out, an' ye don't mek me, nor any one ilse nayther!" Then came a bang of a door, followed by retreating footsteps. Mary had gone aloft ! It was a useless attempt, for whenever I appeared in the kitchen she vanished into a closet, or down the cellar stairs. She is a more reluctant sitter than a certain Boston minister.

A year ago John had a small yellow mongrel for a pet, which used to follow him around lesser Cambridge, but which he seldom brought up to the yard with him. He was greatly attached to this creature ; and the story of the animal's death is most pathetic. It was early one Sunday morning, and the little dog was on his way to Harvard Square to call on an acquaintance. While crossing Main Street, he unfortunately got in front of an electric car and was bisected. For some hours the remains lay in the gutter exposed to the view of the passing church-goers ; and then somebody went down and told John. In a few minutes he was seen coming up the street, trundling an old wheel-barrow covered with a faded hearth-rug. A mob of small boys swarmed around him, now forging ahead, and now lagging behind, like the followers of the "pied piper" of Hamlin town. Poor old John shuffled along behind the barrow, which marked a zigzag path on the hot, dusty road.

On reaching the scene of the disaster, he tenderly lifted the two remains into the wheel-barrow, covered them with the rug, and shambled away, followed by a silent and awe-struck *cortége.*

There was a sad funeral that afternoon at the house of the Orange-man, and what was left of the poor little yellow dog was buried in the back yard.

This singular tenderness for dumb animals is peculiar to the Irish race. A man who will break his neighbor's head with a shillelah, and then go home and get drunk to celebrate the victory, will sit up all night crying over a lame chicken.

But this was to be a short sketch, therefore I must be done. John's stories and adventures are sufficient to fill a large volume; but I must leave them for the personal investigation of the reader, if he be interested to make a further study of the hero.

Though not exactly in the prime of life, he has still many happy years before him. The time will never come when Harvard will close her doors to him. He is the one privileged character that is allowed to pass unmolested the signs, " Pedlers, Beggars, Traders, and Book-agents are not allowed in this Building." In bidding him farewell, let me propose the celebrated toast, given at an Irish dinner, " Long life to him, and may he live to ate the chicken that scratches over his grave! " He has served us faithfully, and will continue to do so as long as he is able to push the hand-cart; and when at last he is too old and feeble to attend to his business, he will come occasionally to the yard and sit in the sun on the steps of Matthews Hall, and his name will be enrolled on the records of the University as

JOHN LOVETT, *Emeritus.*

THE END.